ENDANGERED ISLAND ANIMALS

Dave Taylor

Crabtree Publishing Company

Endangered Animals Series
Text and photographs by Dave Taylor

To my grandparents, who encouraged my interests

Editor-in-chief
Bobbie Kalman

Writing team
Dave Taylor
Bobbie Kalman
Janine Schaub
David Schimpky

Editors
Janine Schaub
David Schimpky

Cover mechanicals
Rose Campbell

Design and computer layout
Antoinette "Cookie" DeBiasi

Photographs
Jim Bryant: 10 (top), 18 (both)
Diane Majumdar: 29

Separations and film
EC Graphics Ltd.

Printer
Worzalla Publishing

Published by
Crabtree Publishing Company

350 Fifth Avenue	360 York Road, RR4	73 Lime Walk
Suite 3308	Niagara-on-the-Lake	Headington
New York	Ontario, Canada	Oxford OX3 7AD
N.Y. 10118	L0S 1J0	United Kingdom

Cataloguing in Publication Data
Taylor, Dave, 1948-
    Endangered island animals

(The endangered animals series)
Includes index.
ISBN 0-86505-532-7 (library bound) ISBN 0-86505-542-4 (pbk.)
Imported predators, overhunting, and habitat destruction are some of the problems faced by endangered island wildlife.

1. Island fauna - Juvenile literature. 2. Endangered species - Juvenile literature. 3. Wildlife conservation - Juvenile literature. I. Title. II. Series: Taylor, Dave, 1948-
The endangered animals series.

QL111.T39 1993   j591.9'1   **LC93-6147**

Contents

The world's islands

Islands are pieces of land surrounded by water. They are found in the world's oceans, lakes, and rivers. There are islands that are small enough to cross in a few jumps and some that are so large that it takes more than a day to get from one side to another by car. The continent of Australia is an example of a very large island. Some islands are cold, bleak places; others are warm, comfortable homes to a variety of plants and animals.

Volcanic islands

When a volcano is formed at sea, lava pours out onto the ocean floor. If enough lava builds up, it will eventually appear above the surface of the water as a **volcanic island**. The Hawaiian, Galapagos, and Seychelles islands were all created in this way. Hawaii's biggest island is still enlarged each year by active volcanoes. Some islands, which were once huge volcanic islands, are slowly being worn away and are washing back into the sea. The small island of Laysan in Hawaii is one of these.

Continental islands

Continental islands are large pieces of land that have broken away from continents. Madagascar, for example, was once part of Africa. Today it lies 250 miles (400 kilometers) off the east African coast.

Coral and barrier islands

Coral islands are pieces of land that are made up of coral, a material secreted by tiny sea animals. **Barrier islands** are formed when rivers carry sand and gravel to the edge of the sea. As these materials wash along the shoreline, long, thin islands are created.

Island animals

Wind and water were responsible for carrying many mainland plants and animals to their island homes. Once these animals found themselves in their island habitats, some developed into different species, whereas others adapted to their new island homes.

Crocodiles, such as the Australian freshwater crocodile shown above, have become rare everywhere they live. In the past they were killed for their skins, which were used for purses, belts, and boots.

Animals in danger

In recent years people have forced many species of animals to struggle for survival. Hunting, farming, and the loss of wilderness areas have made life difficult and sometimes impossible for thousands of species of animals.

Terms of endangerment

Worldwide conservation groups use various terms to describe animals in distress. Animals that are **extinct** have not been seen in the wild for over 50 years. Animals referred to as **endangered** are likely to die out if their situation is not improved. **Threatened** animals are endangered in some areas where they live. Animals that are **vulnerable** may soon move into the endangered category if the causes that put them into danger are not corrected. **Rare** animals are species with small populations that may be at risk.

Threats to island animals

Island animals are especially at risk because they cannot easily move to other locations when they face problems. They are surrounded by water! Some of the animals in this book were hunted almost to extinction for their meat or just for sport. Others died because they could not cope with new animals that were brought to the islands by settlers. Due to the efforts made by conservation groups, there is now hope that many endangered island animals will once again grow in number and face a better future.

Strict laws now protect crocodiles from being overhunted.

Green sea turtles

The green sea turtle is descended from an ancient family of reptiles that lived two hundred million years ago, when dinosaurs still walked the earth. Today this reptile looks much the same as it did ninety million years ago.

Easy targets

Green sea turtles like to swim around shallow islands and coral reefs looking for plants and algae. Their plant diet leaves them without essential vitamins, such as vitamin D, which they absorb by basking in the sun.

When turtles feed in the water or bask on a sunny beach, they are easy to capture. In the past these slow-moving creatures were a ready source of food for native island peoples and European explorers. Up to 100 turtles a day could be caught by a single fisherman! By the year 1620 these huge reptiles were already becoming rare. In some parts of the world, sea turtles are still a major source of food for island peoples.

Perfect for nesting

Lined with palm trees and white sand, tropical and subtropical island beaches are perfect nesting areas for green sea turtles. Unfortunately, the same locations that the turtles find appealing are also popular with tourists and developers. Areas that were once perfect nesting spots for green sea turtles are now built up with hotels, resorts, and condominiums.

Preparing their nests at night

During the nesting season, green sea turtle mothers swim ashore at night to find suitable nesting spots above the high-tide mark on a sandy beach. Each mother digs pits and lays nearly one hundred leathery eggs into them. She then covers her nests with sand. Turtle mothers make up to ten nighttime trips to the same area to lay more eggs. After they have laid their eggs, they never return to their nests.

The dangerous journey

Two months later, all the eggs begin to hatch, and the little turtles dig themselves out of the sand to begin their journey to the sea. As they slowly make their way across the beach, raccoons, herons, opossums, and other predators wait patiently for a tasty treat of tender turtles!

Even the hatchlings that make it to the sea are not safe. Many are eaten by sharks and barracudas. Only one baby in a hundred will survive to adulthood. Those that survive their youth disappear for two years and return to the island when they have grown into adults.

Hope for turtles

Today there are eight species of sea turtles in the world, and all are listed as either endangered or vulnerable. To improve the green sea turtle's chances of survival, nesting sites are marked and guarded by concerned people. In some places, turtle eggs are collected, hatched in laboratories, and the baby turtles are returned to the sea. Many people are working hard to make sure that these remarkable reptiles do not become extinct.

Length: 30-62 inches (76-157 centimeters)
Weight: 120-200 pounds (54-91 kilograms)
Height: 7-12 inches (18-30 centimeters)
Where they live: Tropical and subtropical islands

Unfortunately, there are still places where green sea turtle soup is a popular dish. The soup is made from the turtle's fat, which is green and gives the turtle its name. The serving of turtle soup is now discouraged in most island resorts.

(above) The domed shell of the Galapagos tortoise offers protection from the dogs, cats, rats, and pigs that are the natural enemies of tortoises. Unfortunately, in the past, even the shell of the tortoise could not protect it from the sailors who killed thousands for their meat. Between 1811 and 1844, 15,000 tortoises were carried off the islands to be eaten by sailors.

(left) The Aldabra giant tortoise that lives in the Seychelles has suffered less at the hands of people than its Galapagos cousin. The island locals have a great reverence for this tortoise and have protected it over the years.

Giant tortoises

If you crouched down on all fours, you could disappear under the empty shell of a giant tortoise. This enormous member of the turtle family is a land-dwelling reptile that rarely ventures into the water. Its stubby elephant-like legs are better suited for walking than for swimming. Tortoises move their great weight along very slowly—at a rate of about four miles (6.5 kilometers) per day!

Distant cousins

The tortoise has 39 relatives around the world, but none grow as large as two island species. One species, the Aldabra tortoise, is found on the Seychelles, a group of islands that are located in the Indian Ocean. The other group of tortoises, the more endangered of the two, lives on the Galapagos Islands off the coast of Ecuador in South America. **Galapagos** actually means "tortoises" in Spanish. The name was given to the islands because once thousands of these animals lived there.

Drifted away

Scientists agree that the Aldabra and Galapagos tortoises are related and share a common ancestry, but no one is certain how they arrived in two such distant places. Most people think that the tortoises drifted across the sea from their mainland homes. Over time, they slowly developed into new species in their distant locations.

Hungry sailors

Two centuries ago whaling ships regularly stopped at the Galapagos to collect food. The slow-moving giant tortoises were easily captured and loaded aboard the ships. The sailors kept them below decks and killed them when their food supplies ran out.

Rat attack!

When the ships landed, the black rats that were on board darted ashore at night. They quickly multiplied, and soon there were thousands of these rodents on the islands. They preyed on small animals and feasted on the eggs and hatchlings of the giant tortoises. It was not long before some tortoise species became extinct.

Protection for tortoises

In 1959 the government of Ecuador made a decision to protect giant tortoises and other endangered animals and plants on the Galapagos Islands. Perhaps with the increased world interest in saving giant tortoises, these gentle giants will be around to be admired by future generations.

Aldabra giant tortoise
Length: 55 inches (140 centimeters)
Weight: 559 pounds (254 kilograms)
Where it lives: Seychelles Islands

Galapagos tortoise
Length: 42 inches (110 centimeters)
Weight: 330-440 pounds (150-200 kilograms)
Where it lives: Galapagos Islands

Lemurs

Lemurs are monkey-like animals that live on the island of Madagascar. Fifty million years ago, the island of Madagascar was still part of the mainland of Africa. Gradually, over millions of years, Madagascar broke away from the mainland and drifted slowly out into the Indian Ocean. The lemurs that lived on that piece of land became separated from all the other lemurs in Africa. Without competition for food, the lemurs on the island thrived, whereas their African relatives all died off. Today lemurs can only be found in Madagascar.

Loads of lemurs

Long ago there were many kinds of lemurs living on Madagascar. Some were as small as mice, whereas others were as large as giant orangutans. When Europeans arrived on the island two hundred years ago, they changed the **ecosystem** by farming the land and bringing in domestic animals. As the ecosystem was altered, 14 species of lemurs became extinct.

Food from the forest

Many lemurs spend their entire lives in the tops of trees. With their handlike feet and long front arms, they expertly swing from branch to branch. Lemurs do not use their hands to pick leaves or fruit. Instead, they pull the branches to their mouth and eat directly from them. Other lemurs live on the ground and eat insects and vegetables.

Different eating habits

Many of the smaller lemurs gather food by night, whereas the larger ones search for food during the day. One species, the lesser mouse lemur, eats as much as it can before the dry season arrives. The food it eats is stored as fat in its tail. The lemur then finds a hole or rock crevice and hibernates there until the rains come again. During this time its thick tail keeps it nourished.

Baby acrobats

Lemur mothers are pregnant for two months. They usually give birth to one baby. While the baby is small, it remains

Lemurs rarely leave their treetop homes. Their hands and feet are uniquely adapted to this lifestyle.

firmly clasped to its mother's front with its legs wrapped around her waist and its fingers grasping the hair on her shoulders. No matter what jumps, twists, and turns the mother makes, the baby is able to hold on tightly. With their masklike face coloring, older lemur babies resemble horse jockeys as they ride along on their mothers' backs.

Still facing dangers

Today 22 species of lemurs remain on Madagascar. Some of these species are endangered, but all risk losing their habitats to logging and farming. Fortunately, many people are showing concern for lemurs, and special parks are being set aside for these animals.

Length: 10-59 inches (25-150 centimeters)
Weight: 2.3 ounces-22 pounds (65 grams-10 kilograms)
Where they live: Madagascar

Endangered Hawaiian birds

Thousands of years ago, several species of birds arrived on the Hawaiian Islands and made them their home. Most of these birds thrived because they had no natural island predators.

When Europeans started settling on the islands, they brought foreign animals with them. The dogs, cats, and mongooses killed many of the island birds. Farm animals, such as goats, pigs, and rabbits, ate the vegetation in which the birds made their nests.

European hunters

Animals were not the only dangers the birds faced. European settlers hunted ducks and geese for sport. Using guns, they killed off huge numbers of birds. Many species became extinct. Other species came close to extinction, but are now protected by the law.

Unfortunately, some of the non-native mammals that now live on the Hawaiian Islands eat the eggs and young of the nene. Many nene are raised in zoos so they can be protected while they are young. They are later released as adults, such as the bird below.

The Laysan duck

On the tiny Hawaiian island of Laysan lives one of the most endangered ducks in the world—the Laysan duck. This bird, sometimes called the Laysan teal, almost became extinct when rabbits were brought into its island habitat.

After the rabbits were removed in 1926, the number of Laysan ducks slowly began to recover. By 1957 scientists believed that between 400 and 600 ducks were living on the island. Their future looked bright. Unfortunately, a hurricane in 1963 killed many birds, putting the Laysan duck's survival in jeopardy again.

Mysteriously, today's Laysan duck population goes up and down between a high of 600 and a low of 200 birds. Although there are many theories, no one is sure why there are such wild swings in the population of this duck.

Laysan is now part of the Hawaiian Islands National Wildlife Refuge, and the Laysan duck is fully protected by state laws. Visitors need a special permit to view the duck in its natural habitat. Laysan ducks that live in zoos around the world may eventually be used to help save the wild island population. There are presently 150 ducks living and breeding in captivity.

The Laysan duck likes to wade across the island's shallow ponds, feeding on insects, flies, and tiny forms of marine life.

The nene

The nene is the official state bird of Hawaii. In the past this gooselike bird lived on the remote mountain slopes of the Hawaiian islands. It was overhunted by humans and eaten by the dogs that were brought to the island. Mongooses also killed the birds and ate their eggs and young. By 1949 only 50 nene were left in the whole world, and most of them lived in captivity!

The government of Hawaii began breeding programs in an attempt to save the nene but, when these birds were returned to the wild, they were killed by mongooses. Today there are 200 nene on the island of Hawaii and 100 on Maui, but many more of these birds live in zoos.

Laysan duck
Length: 15-17 inches (38-43 centimeters)
Weight: 1 pound (.45 kilograms)
Where it lives: Laysan Island in Hawaii

Nene
Length: 22-26 inches (55-66 centimeters)
Weight: 3-5 pounds (1.3-2.2 kilograms)
Where it lives: Hawaiian Islands

Hawaiian coot

The Hawaiian coot is a type of American coot—a bird that is commonly found near ponds and marshes. It is endangered due to past overhunting and the continuing loss of its wetland habitat. This coot is found on all the main Hawaiian islands, with the greatest number on Maui, Oahu, and Kauai. Today there are between 2000 to 4500 Hawaiian coots in existence.

> **Hawaiian coot**
> **Length**: 13-14 inches (33-36 centimeters)
> **Weight**: 1-1.5 pounds (450-700 grams)
> **Where it lives**: Hawaiian Islands

Hawaiian water birds, such as the coot above, have become endangered because they are losing their wetland habitats. Marshes and ponds are being drained to make way for farms and ranches.

Hawaiian stilt

The Hawaiian stilt, known as the *a'eo* in Hawaiian, is related to the black-necked stilt, a common North American bird. Its survival was uncertain for many years. In 1940 there were fewer than 1000 stilts in Hawaii. Today the number of these stilts has doubled because the birds are protected by effective laws.

Hawaiian stilts nest in colonies on the mudflats. These nests are in shallow depressions in the ground and are lined with stones, twigs, and other debris. In this depression, the female usually lays four eggs. When the chicks hatch, they are well camouflaged. Their downy feathers blend in with their surroundings. Shortly after hatching, the young are able to walk and find their own food.

Hawaiian moorhen or gallinule

The Hawaiian moorhen belongs to the common gallinule family that lives among the marshy reeds of North America. Today this relative is found on only two Hawaiian islands—Kauai and Oahu. At one time, it was also a resident on the bigger islands. The Hawaiian moorhen became endangered because it was a favorite target for hunters. Even though they have been protected by law since 1939, only 1000 of these birds remain in existence.

The Hawaiian moorhen is very secretive by nature and likes to hide in the dense reeds of marshes. Its strange call has often been compared to the cackle of a chicken.

Hawaiian stilt
Length: 16 inches (41 centimeters)
Weight: 12 ounces (340 grams)
Where it lives: Hawaiian Islands

Hawaiian moorhen
Length: 13-14 inches (33-36 centimeters)
Weight: 7.5 ounces (212 grams)
Where it lives: Hawaiian Islands

(right) In state wildlife refuges, Hawaiian stilts are safe from people but not from the dogs, cats, and mongooses that attack their eggs and young.

(below) Native Hawaiians once believed that the Hawaiian moorhen's beak is red because this bird brought people the gift of the sun.

The Galapagos land iguana

There are two types of iguanas on the Galapagos Islands: land and marine iguanas. Both are large lizards. Scientists once thought that these iguanas were related, but the latest evidence shows that they are two different species.

More marine iguanas left

Although marine and land iguanas are similar in many ways, the population of marine iguanas has not suffered, even though both these lizards live on the same islands. By 1970 most of the land iguanas were massacred by either human hunters or animal predators. Perhaps marine iguanas were able to escape from enemies by swimming away.

Drop in numbers

The story of the Galapagos land iguana is similar to that of other endangered island animals. At one time, land iguanas were plentiful on all the Galapagos Islands. When people came to the islands, however, the population of land iguanas dropped drastically.

Human and animal invaders

Settlers brought all kinds of plants and animals with them. Dogs, cats, rats, mice, cattle, pigs, and goats damaged the delicate ecosystem of the islands. Some of these animals preyed on the land iguana or ate its eggs and babies. People also found iguana meat a tasty delicacy.

Eating the food of the iguana

The plant-eating animals that were brought to the islands ate the food on which the land iguana depended. It did not take long for the land iguana population to diminish. Soon this lizard disappeared from all but three of the nineteen Galapagos Islands.

Stay away!

Land iguanas dig roomy burrows in loose soil or ash. Some live in small caves. The male iguana guards its territory well. When another male enters his area, a shoving battle takes place. To show their anger, iguanas inflate their throats. They then lean against each other until one gets tired and decides to leave.

An effort to bring them home

Great efforts are being made to return land iguanas to a few of the islands where they once lived. Iguana hatchlings are born in captivity and are released on islands that have no rats, dogs, or goats. Unfortunately, these islands still contain some cats that may threaten these baby lizards.

Length: 43 inches (110 centimeters)
Where it lives: The Galapagos Islands

(opposite) Both land and marine iguanas look like prehistoric monsters, but the marine iguana has a menacing face, whereas the land iguana seems to be wearing a constant smile. Can you tell which is which? If you guessed that the iguana on top is a land iguana, you are right!

Rothchild's myna

Rothchild's mynas live in the jungles of Bali, an island in Indonesia. They are relatives of the popular talking mynas found in pet stores.

Disappearing habitat

Once these birds numbered in the thousands, but today they are almost extinct. Much of their jungle habitat has been cut down to make room for coconut plantations. Rothchild's mynas nest in the hollows of trees. As these trees are cleared away, there are fewer places for these birds to live. Today only about 30 wild Rothchild's mynas survive in this island habitat.

These beautiful myna birds are in grave danger. The lush forests of their island home are being chopped down to make way for plantations.

A symbol of the rich

Caged Rothchild's mynas were once popular pets for the Balinese upper classes and military officials. Unfortunately, some wealthy people still want them as pets. **Poachers**, who hunt endangered wildlife illegally, capture and sell these birds. Although the Rothchild's myna is protected by park wardens, many poachers consider the risk of paying fines or going to jail small compared to the large amounts of money they can make by selling these birds. Sadly, most wild mynas die soon after they are captured.

A world project

By 1971 the Jersey Wildlife Preservation Trust had successfully bred over 200 Rothchild's mynas. Since then, 100 other zoos in the United States, Great Britain, and Indonesia have been taking part in a special program to breed these beautiful birds. Today there are over 1000 Rothchild's mynas in zoos.

The center for the breeding and release of Rothchild's mynas is in the Surabaya Zoo in Java, Indonesia. In 1988 the first three captive birds were released to their native habitat. All three died. In 1990 more birds were set free and, this time, most survived. The released birds boosted the wild myna population by one-third!

Length: 10.5 inches (27 centimeters)
Weight: 2.25-3 ounces (64-85 grams)
Where it lives: The island of Bali

Monk seals

When you think of seals, you probably think of snow and icebergs. Most seals do prefer cold climates, but there is one seal that is at home on the beaches of tropical islands. It is the monk seal.

Fossil records tell us that monk seals originally lived around islands in the Caribbean Sea. About 15 million years ago, some migrated to the Mediterranean Sea and some to the Hawaiian Islands.

Vanishing monks

The Caribbean monk seal is believed to be extinct. It was hunted for its fat, called **blubber**, and has not been sighted since 1952. There are fewer than 500 monk seals living in the Mediterranean. Scientists feel that their chances of survival are low because of the large number of boats in the Mediterranean area. The population of the Hawaiian monk seal is also decreasing because of human interference in its habitat.

The Hawaiian monks

Hawaiian monk seals have favorite islands to which they return each year for the purpose of breeding. Female monk seals gather together to meet their mates. Between the middle of March and the end of May, pregnant females give birth to pups. The baby seals are born in the shelter of shrubs on isolated beaches.

Monk seals love to splash around in the tropical waters of Hawaii. They are in danger of extinction because of sharks and human activities such as boating and fishing.

Rich milk

Baby monk seals weigh 35 pounds (16 kilograms) at birth but, in only 17 days, they double their weight. In six weeks, they double their weight again! This tremendous weight gain is due to the rich milk of their mothers. The mother loses four pounds (two kilograms) for every two pounds (one kilogram) her pup gains.

Dangers all around

Sharks are the main enemy of monk seals, but many pups also die because of humans. Fishing boats and larger ships often scare off monk seal mothers, who leave their pups to fend for themselves in dangerous seas.

A questionable future

In the 1950s there were approximately 1200 Hawaiian monk seals counted. Since then, their numbers have decreased. Fortunately, Hawaiian monk seals have a good chance of survival. They live in remote areas and are protected by law. Young females that are abandoned or injured are captured by humans and nursed back to health before they are released into the wild. All these measures help, but one oil spill could wipe out the entire species!

Length: 84-92 inches (214-234 centimeters)
Weight: 381-595 pounds (173-270 kilograms)
Where they live: The coasts of the Hawaiian Islands and the Mediterranean Sea

(above) The mouflon is covered by curly reddish brown wool. In winter this wool becomes thicker and grows darker in color. Mouflons have a good chance of survival because special parks have been created so that these sheep can remain safe from hunters.

The mouflon

The mouflon is the only wild sheep in Europe. It lives on the large Mediterranean islands of Cyprus, Corsica, and Sardinia. Mouflons can be found in the rocky and mountainous regions of these islands as well as in some of the forests. They feed on the grass and low herbs that grow in the rocky terrain.

Rams and ewes

Male mouflons are called **rams.** They have long, curved horns. Female mouflons are called **ewes.** They have no horns. For most of the year, rams live in separate herds from the ewes and their young. During the breeding season, however, rams lead the herds.

Rams fight one another for grazing territory by banging their foreheads together until one ram surrenders. They rarely get hurt because their thick horns offer excellent protection.

Strong legs and keen eyesight

Mouflons are swift runners over rough terrain. They can easily outrun natural enemies such as the wolf, fox, and wildcat. Natural enemies, however, are not a problem for the mouflon anymore. Most have been killed off by hunters.

Hunters are the mouflon's worst enemy. They kill this sheep for its meat. Although the mouflon has no defense against guns, its keen eyesight helps it spot hunters as far as 1.5 miles (2.5 kilometers) away!

Recovering numbers

Despite the speed and sharp eyesight of the mouflon, this sheep was nearly hunted to extinction. To save the remaining mouflons, strict hunting laws were passed by the governments of the islands on which they live. National parks, such as the Paphos Forest area in Cyprus, allow mouflons to live and breed in safety. Recently the mouflon was brought into Germany and other European countries. As a result of these efforts, the mouflon population is steadily increasing throughout Europe as well as on the Mediterranean islands.

Length: 47 inches (120 centimeters)
Height: 26-28 inches (65-70 centimeters)
Where it lives: Corsica, Sardinia, Cyprus, and some European countries

The American crocodile

Although crocodiles sometimes pose a threat to people, people are much more of a threat to crocodiles. Hunters in tropical and subtropical areas have nearly destroyed all of them. Between 1950 and 1980, so many of these creatures were killed for their leather that all crocodile species became endangered. Today the American crocodile is a very rare reptile.

At one time American crocodiles were found throughout southern Florida, the Caribbean Islands, along the east and west coasts of Mexico, and in Venezuela and Colombia. Today they are almost extinct. The few hundred surviving American crocodiles are now found in Florida's Everglades and the islands that make up the Florida Keys.

Crocodiles have sharp teeth and incredibly powerful jaws. Their prey has little chance of escaping.

Strange connections

Like turtles, crocodiles first appeared during the days of the dinosaurs, some 65 million years ago. Scientists believe that crocodiles belong to the dinosaur family called the **archosaurs**. When you are looking at a crocodile, you are seeing a dinosaur-like creature!

Excellent mothers

When it is time to have young, the female crocodile digs a hole in the ground, lays about 30 eggs, and covers them with rotting vegetation. The heat of the decomposing plants helps keep the eggs at the right temperature. The mother takes care to guard the nest from predators that feed on crocodile eggs.

Breaking out

Crocodile babies break out of their leathery shells with the help of a special egg tooth on their snout. Soon after hatching, the babies shed this tooth. They move to the water where they eat small insects and fish. When these crocodiles become adults, they drift slowly or lie in wait until their prey, which is usually a fish or mammal, swims by. They then quickly clamp down their huge interlocking teeth on their helpless prey.

Conserving the cute

Many people are enthusiastic about the protection of "cute" animals, such as panda bears and baby seals, but are less interested in protecting large, ferocious-looking reptiles such as the American crocodile. Only recently have people begun to realize that American crocodiles are an important part of the food web and should be protected.

Length: 20 feet (6 meters)
Weight: Up to 500 pounds (227 kilograms)
Where it lives: Caribbean islands and the coast of the Gulf of Mexico

Preserving island animals and habitats

When people moved to the islands around the world, they brought with them plants and animals that were not native to their new island homes. These plants and animals often had a devastating effect on the environment.

Wildlife that does not belong to an island ecosystem can kill off food supplies and replace island species. In Australia, for example, non-native rabbits and cane toads have caused serious problems for island wildlife. In Hawaii, mongooses threatened the survival of island birds.

Pets running wild

Many island habitats around the world are also threatened by pets that run wild. Dogs and cats that are loose can behave like wild predators, killing native birds and mammals. If you are a pet owner, keep your animals under supervision and help protect your local environment.

Buying a pet

If you buy a pet, make sure that you know the origin of your new animal. Many exotic animals, such as the Rothchild's myna, have been captured in other countries where they are becoming endangered. If you buy such pets, you could be reducing the populations of island animals.

Making choices

When we go shopping, we make choices about the products we buy. You can help preserve island wildlife by choosing not to purchase illegal island-animal products. Turtle-shell jewelry and crocodile-skin purses are just two examples of such products.

Mongooses, which were brought by the settlers, killed off many species of island birds and reptiles.

Planning a trip

The next time you and your family are taking a vacation, go to an island that has a park or wildlife refuge. By visiting these places, you will be showing that you support nature!

Making a difference

On islands, especially smaller islands, the removal of plants, animals, and beach souvenirs can harm and sometimes permanently change the environment. Even little things like seashells can make a big difference and cause changes to island habitats far more quickly than on mainland areas. Respect wildlife areas by not taking parts of them with you as souvenirs. After all, would you want visitors to your home to take your belongings as keepsakes?

Glossary

algae Tiny plants that live in the ocean

archosaurs The family of dinosaurs to which the crocodile may have belonged

Bali A south Pacific island that is part of Indonesia

barrier island An island that is formed when rivers carry sand and gravel to the sea

blubber The layer of fat found under the skin of some sea mammals such as seals and whales

burrow A hole dug in the ground by an animal in which it lives and hides

Caribbean Relating to the Caribbean Sea and its islands

condominium A building consisting of individually owned apartments

conservation Protection from loss, harm, or waste, especially of natural resources, such as wildlife

continental island An island that has broken away from a continent

coral A hard substance found in tropical ocean areas. It is secreted by small aquatic animals.

coral island An island that is made up of coral

Corsica A Mediterranean island that is a part of France

Cyprus An independent Mediterranean island

delicacy A choice or rare food

ecosystem A community of living things that are connected to one another and to the surroundings in which they live

endangered To be threatened with extinction

environment The setting and conditions in which a living being exists

ewe A female sheep

exotic Belonging to another part of the world; not native

extinct Not in existence; not seen in the wild for over 50 years

flock A gathering of one kind of animal

Galapagos Islands An island group located off the coast of Ecuador in South America

habitat The natural environment of a plant or animal

mudflat A coastal area that is flooded at high tide and exposed at low tide

plantation A large farm where one crop is grown

poacher A person who hunts animals illegally

population The people or animals of an area; the total number of individuals living in a particular area

predator An animal that kills and eats other animals

prey An animal that is hunted by another animal for food

ram A male sheep

range An area over which an animal roams and finds food

rare Uncommon; in danger of becoming extinct

refuge Shelter or protection from danger

Sardinia A large Mediterranean island that is part of Italy

Seychelles Islands An island group located in the Indian Ocean

species A group of related plants or animals that can produce young together

subtropical Relating to areas near tropical regions

threatened Describing wildlife that is endangered in some parts of its habitat

tropical Hot and humid; describing an area close to the equator

volcanic island An island made from the build-up of lava

volcano A cone-shaped mountain built up out of the lava that is ejected from its center

vulnerable Capable of becoming endangered

wetland A marshy freshwater area that is dry for part of the year

Index

4 5 6 7 8 9 0   Printed in USA   2 1 0 9 8 7 6